101 SPOTS

Creative Scripts for Radio, TV & Internet Ads

David K. Jones

Contents

- 101 Spots 1
- Restaurants & Bars 7
  - Restaurant "Best Way to the Heart" 8
  - Café/Candy/Burgers "Car Full of Kids" 9
  - Restaurant "Elvis PBB&B" 10
  - Restaurant/Bar "Freezing" 11
  - Restaurant "Holiday Rush" 12
  - Pizza Shop "Holiday Getaway" 13
  - BBQ "The Real Deal" 14
  - Bar/Nightclub "Little Black Dress" 15
  - Restaurant (Mexican) "North & South" 16
  - Restaurant/Bar/Arcade "Escape the Weather" 17
  - Coffee Shop "Holy Grail" 18
  - Restaurant "Lies" 19
  - Restaurant/Bar "St Patrick's Day" 20
  - Beer Pub "New World" 21
  - Catering "Think Smarter" 22
  - Restaurant/Bar "Girls Night Out" 23
  - Restaurant "Fish Fry" 24
  - Bar "Karaoke" 25
  - Bar/Pub "77 Percent Women" 26
  - Restaurant (Italian) "Taste of Italy" 27
- Professional Services 28
  - Lawyer "Father's Rights" 29
  - Travel Agent "Spring Break" 30
  - Insurance Agent "Vacation Check Up" 31
  - Tax Consultant/Lawyer "Tax Relief" 32
  - Plumbing "Knows Water" 33

Contractor "Disasters" 34
Photographer "Eternal Memories" 35
Manicurist "Flip Flop Ready" 36
Tattoo "Work of Art" 37
Excavating "On the Hole" 38
Mortgage/Bank "Love at First Sight" 39
Computer Repair "Adorable" 40
Hair Salon "Winter Head" 41
Contractor "Quotes" 42
Window/Door Installers "Draft" 43
Heating & Cooling "Root of the Problem" 44
Contracting "Gray Thumb" 45

Retail 46

Flowers "Anytime" 47
Jeweler "What Women Want" 48
Market/Grocery "Katherine Valentine" 49
Furniture Store/Decorator "Why Not Me" 50
Mattress "Who is to Blame" 51
Retail "Shop Local" 52
Western Wear "Look Good" 53
Market Valentine "Your Way" 54
Framing/Print Shops "Plain Walls" 55
Shoe Store "Talk Show" 56
Antique Shop "Memories" 57
Building Supply "Talking Lumber" 58
Guitar or Music Shop "We Got Your Axe" 59
Frame Shop "Dark Night" 60
Nursery/Garden Center "Talking Flowers" 61
Pet/Aquarium Shop "Hi Def" 62
Grocery "Graduation" 63
Nursery "Earth Day" 64

BBQ Grill /Hardware Store "Grilling Tips" 65
T-Shirt Shop "Classy or Crazy" 66
Boutique/Market "Mother's Day" 67
Building/Hardware Store "After Xmas Remodel" 68
Book Store "Amazing Books" 69
Jeweler "Sparkle in Her Eyes" 70
Grocery/Market "What Mom Didn't Do" 71

Medical & Such 72
Dentist/Oral Surgeon "Doctor Speaking" 73
Chiropractor "Tune Up" 74
Health Store "One Body" 75
Body Rejuvenation/Fitness Center "Summer Body" 76
Dentist "Anxieties" 77
Walk-In Clinic "Predict" 78
Elder Homecare "They Were There for You" 79
Dentist "Bad Puns" 80
Vision Shop/Optometrist "Beautiful World" 81
Pharmacy "Cold Confusion" 82

Automotive 83
Auto Dealer "Uncomplicated" 84
Auto Repair "Summer Campaign" 85
Auto Repair "Ouch!" 86
Auto Repair "Double Talk" 87
Auto Repair "Sorry Mechanic" 88
Car Wash "I'm Filthy" 89
Auto Detailing "Spring Cleaning" 90
Auto Dealer "Freeze Out Sale" 91
Auto Body "Charm Bracelet" 92
Auto Salvage "Pull 'em Out" 93
Auto Dealer "No Time for Bull" 94
Rental Car "Summer Wheels" 95

- Custom Wheel & Tires "Invention of the Wheel" 96
- RV Sales & Repair "Get Out of Here" 97

Miscellaneous 98
- Boutique or ANY "Not ONE Thing I Like" 99
- ANY "Subliminal" 100
- Wine/Liquor Store "World of Wines" 101
- Fitness Center "Fireworks" 102
- Appliances "Dream TV Home" 103
- Pools "Splash" 104
- Pools "All Dried Up" 105
- Credit Union "YOU Can Join" 106
- Metal Recycling "A Lot of "*crap" 107
- Bowling "Memories" 108
- Limo "We Keep Secrets" 109
- Cleaners "Holiday Stains" 110
- Locksmith "More than Computers" 111
- Karate School "Every Advantage" 112
- Weight Loss "New Year" 113

About the Author 114

Introduction

I have had the privilege to work at small town stations and at some of the most listened to radio giants in the country. When it comes to commercial advertising, it is all the same. We are trying to get a message to one listener. A message that they will remember and one that they will act on.

We want to:
- Get into the audience's head
- Surprise them with a unique approach
- Keep the main message simple
- Don't overload them with information
- Be MEMORABLE

The scripts I've included in this book can easily be modified for you clients. I hope they will also inspire you create your own.

Good luck and be creative!

David

Restaurants & Bars

Restaurant "Best Way to the Heart"

Title	Best Way to the Heart
Client/Product	Restaurant/Grocery
Voice Gender	Female
Length	:30
Direction	
Suggested Music/SFX	Fun music

They say, the best way to a man's heart is…through his chest with a scalpel or reciprocating saw. Of course, the second-best way is chicken wings. Right now, <u>Wing World</u> has 12 wings for just 7.99! Whether it's for game-days, birthdays or "I-don't-wanna-cook" days, <u>Wing World</u> has your mild to extra spicy heart-pounding wings waiting. And don't forget <u>Wing World</u> has 50 wings for 19 bucks! …now that'll make him sit up and pay attention…then…of course, he'll probably just lie back and nap. <u>Wing World</u> Online at XYZ dot com!

(Easily modified for any food product from pastries to pizza. Works for grocery baking supply sales too)

Café/Candy/Burgers "Car Full of Kids"

Title	Car-full of kids
Client/Product	Cafe-Candy-Burgers
Voice Gender	Male and Female
Length	:30
Direction	Female (frustrated but natural) Male (announcer-ish)
Suggested Music/SFX	(open with kids fighting or arguing SFX)

Female: What a car full! Jessica in the back seat wants ice cream. Tommy insists on a hot dog. . . All I want is a nice cup a coffee

Male: Hey Mom Why don't you just bring them down to <u>Jones Treats</u> where Jessica can get her ice cream, Tommy can get his hotdog and at <u>Jones Treats</u> you can even get your coffee.

Female: Who was that man?

Male: "The Voice of Reason"...and the voice of Jones<u> Treats</u> at (Location).

(Works for Candy Stores, Burger Shops and Cafes. Just substitute menu items. The goal is to relate to harried parents with kids and implant a suggestion on where to go for a "break." The mood is more important than the menu items.)

Restaurant "Elvis PBB&B"

Title	Elvis PBB&B
Client/Product	Restaurant
Voice Gender	Male or Female
Length	:30
Direction	Make 'em hungry
Suggested Music/SFX	Elvis style rock 'n roll

It's legendary. It's delicious...and it was made for the King. The King of Rock 'n Roll. November is national Peanut Butter Lover's Month and all month-long Jones Restaurant will feature the Elvis Peanut Butter, Banana and Bacon Sandwich. Yeah, you can still get <u>delicious burgers and their famous fried chicken.</u> But just imagine a custom-made Peanut Butter and Banana sandwich with Bacon...did I mention BACON? *Oh, yeah!*

The Elvis Peanut Butter, Banana and BACON sandwich only at Jones Restaurant (location) and only in November!

Restaurant/Bar "Freezing"

Title	Freezing
Client/Product	Restaurant, Bar, (?)
Voice Gender	Male or Female
Length	:30
Direction	Mock seriousness
Suggested Music/SFX	Chilling wind effects

:15 Friend

Remember that old friend who said he'd buy you dinner "when hell freezes over?"…well with the temperatures outside, TODAY must be your lucky day! While it's still frozen over get to <u>JONES PLACE</u>. And don't forget to bring that old friend of yours to <u>JONES PLACE (location)</u>

:15 Mama

Mama said there'd be days like this…Mama also said that when those days were colder than penguin poop you should head to <u>JONES PLACE</u>. God bless, dear mama! Make mama happy, warm up at <u>JONES PLACE (location)</u> today.

Restaurant "Holiday Rush"

Title	Holiday Rush
Client/Product	Restaurant
Voice Gender	Male or Female
Length	:30
Direction	Start hurried then relax
Suggested Music/SFX	Fast music then more relaxing

(Hurried delivery and hurried music) Get the kids to school, get to work, do some work, make a gift list, leave work, pick up the kids, drop the kids off, shop for gifts, go home. Forgot anything? Oh yeah…Dinner! *(more relaxing delivery and music)* Jones Restaurant has you covered. All the great food you love at Jones Restaurant is waiting for you enjoy after a busy day. Don't feel like eating out? No problem…call ahead to pick up your favorite food for the crew. This holiday season don't forget dinner…and don't forget Jones Restaurant. (location) (web site or phone number)

You can add specialty items like "pizza" or "fried chicken"…but don't get bogged down listing menu items….the idea is to get into the head of a busy adult and sell the idea of "eating out or take-away"…not necessarily the specifics of the menu.

Pizza Shop "Holiday Getaway"

Title	Holiday Getaway
Client/Product	Pizza Shop
Voice Gender	Male or Female
Length	:30
Direction	Sarcastic then enthused
Suggested Music/SFX	Traffic sound effects or "hustle-bustle" music then transition into Italian music.

The holiday season is great: Home, family, shopping for gifts and running around from store to store. Yeah, all that junk. Now don't get me wrong, I like all that holiday stuff. Just sometimes I get overwhelmed and need to get away. Maybe to Italy! Doesn't that sound nice? ...a quick Italian getaway! That's when I call Jones Pizza. They deliver the taste of Italy right to my door. No cooking, no stress...just a quick Italian vacation courtesy of Jones Pizza, call them at XXX-XXXX. Online at XYZ.com. Come on, you deserve it!

BBQ "The Real Deal"

Title	**The Real Thing**
Client/Product	BBQ
Voice Gender	Male or Female
Length	:30
Direction	Passionate. Possibly southern drawl.
Suggested Music/SFX	Fairly slow blues guitar works well

Some say the best barbecue comes from smokehouses in the Carolinas. Other say you'll find it down in Texas. Still others claim St Louis or Memphis. They're ALL wrong. The best barbecue can be found right here in (your town) at Jones BBQ. Meaty fall-off-the bone BBQ ribs, pulled pork, chicken and all those authentic fixin's. I'll be you can almost taste it. Well don't "ALMOST taste it" come down to (location) and taste Jones BBQ in person. You KNOW you want to. Jones BBQ, the REAL thing. Online at XYZ.com

Bar/Nightclub "Little Black Dress"

Title	Little Black Dress
Client/Product	Nightclub-bar
Voice Gender	Male
Length	:30
Direction	Sexy
Suggested Music/SFX	Music appropriate to the nightclub

Nothing makes a girl look sexier than a little black dress...unless she's wearing her little black dress at Jones Nightclub.

Oh yeah! ... Little Black Dress Fridays at Jones Nightclub

We'll keep the music movin' and the drinks flowin'. Fridays at Jones Nightclub are legendary, so, girls, slip into your little black dress and head to Jones Nightclub on Friday...and guys...well...we know where you'll be headin' to on Friday!

Jones Nightclub.s Little Black Dress Fridays...(location)

(This works with any style nightclub or bar. Just change the music. It can also work on any day of the week...possibly on Wednesdays instead of Ladies night. Also the bar can give a discounts on drinks or apps to ladies wearing "little black dresses.")

Restaurant (Mexican) "North & South"

Title	North & South
Client/Product	Mexican Restaurant
Voice Gender	Male
Length	:30
Direction	Fairly rapid delivery/ style of Denis Leary
Suggested Music/SFX	Mexican music

So on my last trip down in Mexico my old buddy, Frank, takes me to this little restaurant he says has the best food south of the Border. It was great, but I said to Frank, it's almost as good as Jones Cantina. He asked where in Mexico could he find Jones Cantina. I said (LOCATION.) Frank gave me that look he gives me sometimes. So the first thing we did when we got back home was head to Jones Cantina. Frank was convinced. And if you ever run into Frank and ask him where to find the best Mexican food, he'll tell you the best food north AND south of the border is at Jones Cantina (Location)

Restaurant/Bar/Arcade "Escape the Weather"

Title	Escape the weather
Client/Product	Restaurant, Bar, Arcade
Voice Gender	Male or Female
Length	:15
Direction	A little "over-acting"!
Suggested Music/SFX	Weather effects

:15 Weatherman

Hi Radio Listeners...I'm an unlicensed meteorologist with this report...the weather is officially "poopy". You could stay home wrap yourself in boredom...or head to JONES PLACE and have some fun... snowballs outside mean fun inside at JONES PLACE.

:15 Man Up

You have a wardrobe of the warmest clothes science can create. You own a vehicle that get you anywhere anytime. So why are hiding? Man up... or woman up. Get to JONES PLACE. When the weather intense the FUN is intense at JONES PLACE.

:15 Brave Text

Neither wind, nor snow nor slushy streets will keep our brave citizens from their destiny: JONES PLACE! Escape the weather and embrace the fun at JONES PLACE! (Location)

(If your client has specials or entertainment...add those and you've got a nice 30 second ad.)

Coffee Shop "Holy Grail"

Title	Holy Grail
Client/Product	Coffee Shop
Voice Gender	Male or Female
Length	:30
Direction	Dramatic
Suggested Music/SFX	Medieval music.

For years it has been searched for the world over. One sip is supposed to change you forever. A seemingly impossible quest. No, not the Holy Grail.... the perfect cup of coffee!

At last it's been found...at Jones Coffee Shop!

Each cup is lovingly prepared for every knight and lady. Crusades have been fought for less! Come experience what many call the Holy Grail of Coffee...at Jones Coffee Shop, location.

Restaurant "Lies"

Title	Lies
Client/Product	Restaurant
Voice Gender	Male or Female
Length	:30
Direction	Dramatic
Suggested Music/SFX	Dramatic

You ask her if she wants to eat out tonight, and she says, "No" and that she'll just "whip something up."

SHE IS A LIAR.

She REALLY WANTS to go out to dinner. The last thing she desires is to cook. She's just being nice.

DO NOT BELIEVE HER.

Take her to Jones Restaurant. No Shopping, No cooking, No Cleanup.

Do the right thing. Take her to Jones Restaurant, Location...and don't believe her lies.

Restaurant/Bar "St Patrick's Day"

Title	St Pats
Client/Product	Bar, Pub or Restaurant
Voice Gender	Male or Female
Length	:30
Direction	Irish accent if you've got one!
Suggested Music/SFX	Irish music

Some people still haven't recovered from last year's party...TOO BAD, it's time to do it again! Take St Patrick's Day off and come out to Jones Pub! It's the BIGGEST party in (location)! Cold Beer, great food and all of your friends. St Patrick's Day at Jones Pub is the stuff legends are made of! Come out all day this St. Patrick's Day. You might want to take the NEXT day off too!

Beer Pub "New World"

Title	New World
Client/Product	Beer Pub
Voice Gender	Male or Female
Length	:30
Direction	Sincere
Suggested Music/SFX	

There was a time when all beer tasted about the same. People chose their favorite brew based on TV commercials and what Dad, did or did <u>not</u> drink.

Times have changed. Beer has changed.

Now we enjoy a world of flavor. From rich hearty stouts to clean fruity ciders. <u>Jones Pub</u> is your connection to the new world of beer and the work of a new breed of brew masters. Drop by <u>Jones Pub (location)</u> and sample our constantly revolving selection of beers. It may take a while but with the help of <u>Jones Pub</u>, they hope to serve you up every style beer in the world, one-beer-at-a-time!

Catering "Think Smarter"

Title	Think Smarter
Client/Product	Catering
Voice Gender	Male or Female
Length	:30
Direction	sincere
Suggested Music/SFX	

So you've got that big get-together coming up.

You could prepare all the food yourself, but, seriously...do you REALLY want to do that?

Of course, you could make it Pot-Luck...but with your luck, everyone would just end up bringing a Jell-O salad with marshmallows.

Think smarter. Call Jones Catering and let them handle everything. From a small business meeting to the largest family reunion. Jones Catering will handle it all. Appetizers through desert.

Jones Catering, online at XYZ.com or call XXX-XXXX

Restaurant/Bar "Girls Night Out"

Title	Girls Night Out
Client/Product	Restaurant/Bar/Club
Voice Gender	Female
Length	:30
Direction	Fun
Suggested Music/SFX	Exciting music.

Aren't you due for a little "girl time?" Jones Grill wants you to gather your girlfriends, co-workers and even mom for Girls Night Out this Wednesday. Special prices for the girls, special appetizers and a guaranteed great night of fun with old and new friends! So get on the phone and get the girls together for Girls Night Out at Jones Grill this Wednesday. Jones Grill (Location)

Restaurant "Fish Fry"

Title	**Fish Fry**
Client/Product	Restaurant
Voice Gender	Male
Length	:30
Direction	Rough and raspy
Suggested Music/SFX	Bell, seagulls and sea faring music.

(ROUGH Voice like a pirate or old salty sailor…raspy, deep)
(sound effects of ship bell and seagulls)

I've sailed the seven seas and have been to many ports. Oh, the sites I've seen! But the best seafood I've ever put in me mouth is the delicious fish they prepare at <u>Joneses'</u> Friday Fish Fry. Always crispy on the outside and fresh and tender on the inside. They know how to handle their fish! I think there's a mermaid in the kitchen, but I can't be sure. And I never go away hungry. Big portions and all the fixin's that make a fish fry fantastic.

Set sail this Friday and join me and the lads at <u>Joneses (location)</u>. I'll be lookin' fer that mermaid!

Bar "Karaoke"

Title	Karaoke
Client/Product	Bar/Super club
Voice Gender	Male or Female
Length	:30
Direction	
Suggested Music/SFX	

Inside every average schmoe...there's a hidden Rock Star.

Jones Bar & Grille wants to let the world see and hear the rock star in <u>you</u>!

Join us every Wednesday Night when average schmoes perform their favorite songs at Jones Bar & Grille. Come on out and show the world your stuff. Bring your friends and be the dream band you've always known you could be.

Gather the gang... come as you are, or show up in your rock star clothes. This Wednesday YOU are the rock star, at Jones Bar & Grille.

(Location)

Bar/Pub "77 Percent Women"

Title	**77 percent for women**
Client/Product	Bar/Pub
Voice Gender	Female
Length	:30
Direction	
Suggested Music/SFX	

Statistics show that, on average, women earn 77 percent of what men do.

At Jones Pub we want to do something about that. Ladies, this Wednesday, come to <u>Jones Pub</u> and we will only charge you 77 percent of your total bill.

Bring your friends and have a girl's night out at <u>Jones Pub</u> this Wednesday.

All women over 21 pay just 77 percent of their bill. Its just a little way to equal things out. <u>Jones Pub (Location)</u>

Restaurant (Italian) "Taste of Italy"

Title	Taste Italy
Client/Product	Italian Restaurant
Voice Gender	Male or Female
Length	:30
Direction	Smooth and mellow
Suggested Music/SFX	Italian music (elegant)

The rolling hills of Tuscany. The winding roads of the Amalfi Coast. An amazing café on the streets of Rome. We've brought all that Italy has to offer into Jones Italian Restaurant. Stroll into our little bit of Italy and start off with perfect light appetizer. Maybe a glass of vintage Italian Wine. Then from the northern to southernmost provinces of Italy choose your entree from a delicious selection of regional favorites.

Don't just dream the dream of Italy. Taste Italy! Jones Italian Restaurant, (Location).

Professional Services

Lawyer "Father's Rights"

Title	Fathers Rights
Client/Product	Lawyer
Voice Gender	Male and announcer
Length	:30
Direction	Real and honest
Suggested Music/SFX	

(Male voice)
I wanna be fair
She deserves a fair deal...but Hey so do I
I don't want to take her to the cleaners
But I have a feeling I'm about to get dry cleaned
Oh yeah...she'll probably get custody of my tailor

Announcer:
If you've been thinking about divorce you need to take control right now. The Law Offices of Jones & Jones believes in equality in Divorce. They'll prevent her from taking an upper hand.

The Law Offices of Jones & Jones consultations are free. Call (phone number)

Travel Agent "Spring Break"

Title	Spring Break
Client/Product	Travel agent
Voice Gender	Male or Female
Length	:30
Direction	Upbeat
Suggested Music/SFX	Wind effect. Tropical music.

(sound of cold wind)

You've been working hard…and so has Mother Nature. It's been a cold winter and you're exhausted. Don't you deserve a break? A <u>SPRING</u> break!

(tropical music)

Jones Travel has been arranging needed spring breaks for deserving people for years. Whether it's a sunny beach getaway, a scenic cruise or an escape to a secluded cabin, Jones Travel can find the right destination to fit your dreams <u>and</u> your budget. Give them a call or just drop in at (location). Jones Travel, your first stop on your way to your Spring Break!

Insurance Agent "Vacation Check Up"

Title	Vacation check up
Client/Product	Insurance Agent
Voice Gender	Male or Female
Length	:30
Direction	Sincere
Suggested Music/SFX	

Going on Vacation?
Route planned? Check!
Bags Packed.? Check!
Car Insurance? ....Not Checked?

Before you head out this summer make sure to check your auto insurance. Do you have all the coverage you need? Rental car replacement? Road assistance and towing? Let Jones Insurance give you the confidence you need to relax on the road and at your final vacation destination. Whether it's an insurance checkup or a new policy that suites your needs. Jones Insurance is your first stop on your vacation agenda. Jones Insurance (Location/number and/or website)

Tax Consultant/Lawyer "Tax Relief"

Title	Tax Relief
Client/Product	Lawyer or Tax consultant
Voice Gender	Male or Female
Length	:30
Direction	serious
Suggested Music/SFX	

It's that time when lots of people are excited about getting tax refunds, but is that the last thing on your mind? Are you worried about paying off your old tax debt to the IRS? Are you frightened of tax liens, property seizures, and your family's wages being garnished? It IS a possibility...but there is tax relief. Visit the understanding professionals at Jones & Jones. The IRS will settle for pennies on the dollar but you must know where to start and the best place to start is Jones & Jones. Call us at XXX-XXXX or visit us online at XXX.com

Plumbing "Knows Water"

Title	Predict
Client/Product	Walk in clinic
Voice Gender	Male or Female
Length	:30
Direction	Sincere
Suggested Music/SFX	Easy going.

Some things you can't predict. Like that trampoline accident on a Saturday morning, or finding out after school that someone has been feeling ill all day. Don't worry, Jones Express Clinic is there for you, seven days a week from 9am to 7pm. Make an appointment or just walk in. And at Jones Express Clinic we are here for unexpected emergencies, illness checkups, sports physicals and flu shots. Life is full of surprises but one thing you can predict… is that Jones Express Clinic is always there for you.

Contractor "Disasters"

Title	Disasters
Client/Product	Contracting
Voice Gender	Male or Female
Length	:15
Direction	V1=exaggerated V2=calm
Suggested Music/SFX	See script

:15

Voice 1: Hey look watch me flambé this pork chop like an iron chef

(explosion)

Voice 2: Fire, Water, Natural disasters, even mold

Quick response

Jones Contracting

:15

Voice 1: Don't worry 'bout that hole in the roof, its not gonna rain

(Thunder)

Voice 2: Fire, Water, Natural disasters, even mold

Quick response

Jones Contracting

:15

Voice 1: Get the camcorder and watch this

(Chainsaw)

Voice 1: Timber! *(crash)*

Voice 2: Fire, Water, Natural disasters, even mold

Quick response

Jones Contracting

Photographer "Eternal Memories"

Title	Eternal memories
Client/Product	Photographer
Voice Gender	Male or Female
Length	:30
Direction	Sincere
Suggested Music/SFX	

In everyone's life there are fleeting moments that become eternal memories. Capture those memories with affordable yet astounding photography. Jones Photography specializes in capturing the feel and emotion of the moment. Your special wedding, corporate imaging, breathtaking real estate photos and family portraits that reflect your one-of a kind family. Don't settle for just photos... Let Jones Photography capture the emotion. Online at XYZ.com or call XXX-XXXX

Manicurist "Flip Flop Ready"

Title	Flip Flop Ready
Client/Product	Manicures Pedicures
Voice Gender	Male or Female
Length	:30
Direction	Fun
Suggested Music/SFX	Summer music

Are your feet flip-flop ready? You know what I mean girls...you want to look great in all the sexy summer styles and that includes your fingers and toes. JONES Manicures and Pedicures is a full-service spa specifically for your hands and feet. Now that it's hot...look hot. And for gosh sakes, don't wear socks with your flip-flops!

Before you step outside, step into JONES and get a mani-pedi makeover! Jones Manicures and Pedicures at (Location)

Tattoo "Work of Art"

Title	Work of art
Client/Product	Tattoo
Voice Gender	Male or Female
Length	:30
Direction	Warm
Suggested Music/SFX	

Art is a matter of personal choice. It reflects the artisan's skill and the owner's desire to proudly display that artwork for the world the see. No art is more timeless than body art.

A tattoo can be strong and impactful or light and graceful. Jones Tattoo will work with you and your custom work of art.

Whether you have a unique design that you want to be skillfully interpreted or you want to be inspired by one of Jones Tattoo's in house designs, come see what we have to offer at (Location)

Excavating "On the Hole"

Title	On The Hole
Client/Product	Excavating
Voice Gender	Male or Female
Length	:30
Direction	
Suggested Music/SFX	Can use tractor/bulldozer effects

Sometimes, for some unexpected reason, we find ourselves in a hole. What to do? Call <u>Jones Excavating</u>, we'll <u>fill</u> that hole! Maybe you NEED a hole. We can create a hole too. Trenching, leveling, backfilling…excavating of any kind. <u>Jones Excavating</u> can dig it or fill it! Call <u>Jones Excavating</u> at (Phone Number) or online at (Website). Just remember, "When it comes to holes, <u>Jones Excavating</u> is the best…on the whole!

Mortgage/Bank "Love at First Sight"

Title	Love at first sight
Client/Product	Mortgage
Voice Gender	Male or Female
Length	:30
Direction	Sincere
Suggested Music/SFX	romantic

Remember when you first met it was love at first sight, but now…a relationship that seemed so wonderful is like an anchor. Of course, I'm talking about your Home Loan. Maybe you should consider the R word…. Refinance. With historically low rates, Jones Mortgage can help you refinance and save today before there is any more pain and suffering. Call Jones Mortgage at XXX-XXXXX or online at XYZ.com

Computer Repair "Adorable"

Title	Adorable
Client/Product	Computer Repair
Voice Gender	Male or Female
Length	:30
Direction	
Suggested Music/SFX	Nursey music and upbeat techno music.

(nursery style music)

Remember the day your computer arrived! Everyone in the office gathered round saying how adorable it was, how fast and smart it was.

But with time it's slowed down…

(music winds down)

Now it takes unexpected naps and gets frequent viruses. You need <u>Jones Computers</u>

(upbeat music)

<u>Jones Computers</u> will make your PC feel young again. Free inspection and diagnostics. Even free computer pickup. <u>Jones Computers</u>

Online at XYZ.com or call XXX-XXXX

Hair Salon "Winter Head"

Title	Winter Head
Client/Product	Hair Salon
Voice Gender	Male or Female
Length	:30
Direction	Happy and upbeat
Suggested Music/SFX	Bright music

Everyone's heard of "bed head"...but do you have "Winter head?"

You know, a hair style that looks like you've been in hibernation for the past 6 months. Maybe it's time to spring forward with a fresh new hairstyle.

Jones Salon can give you the look you've been looking for! From a simple spring trim to an amazing spring makeover, call (phone number) for your appointment. Or drop by (location) and talk to our expert stylists at Jones Salon...and get rid of your Winter-head!

Contractor "Quotes"

Title	Quotes
Client/Product	Contractor
Voice Gender	3 voices plus announcer (or can be just 1)
Length	:30
Direction	
Suggested Music/SFX	

V1 Great Barn, but you forgot to put in a door.

V2 Why aren't there any power outlets in the walls.

V3 Nice remodel, but where the refrigerator is supposed to be you put a toilet.

Anncr. Quotes from people who DID NOT us Jones <u>Contracting.</u>

You see <u>Jones</u> knows contracting. From blue print design to final construction and most importantly...REALITY.

<u>Jones Contracting</u> does all the work and the thinking so all you have to do is dream...then enjoy.

<u>Jones Contraction</u>
<u>(phone or website)</u>

If you use just one voice possible use "filter" effect on the first three voices and separate with an electronic "beep"

Window/Door Installers "Draft"

Title	Draft
Client/Product	Window–Door Remodeling
Voice Gender	Male or Female
Length	:30
Direction	Sincere
Suggested Music/SFX	

Do you feel a draft? Maybe it's from those old windows? Or that funky front door? Let the experts at Jones Windows check your home out. They'll find that draft and give you warmth you can see, feel and spend. Energy efficient doors, windows and siding from Jones Windows will not only keep you warmer in the winter and cooler in summer but beautify your home and save you money on energy bills. Get your free estimate…Visit Jones Windows at XYZ.com

Heating & Cooling "Root of the Problem"

Title	Root of the problem
Client/Product	Heating Cooling
Voice Gender	Male or Female
Length	:30
Direction	Sincere
Suggested Music/SFX	

Ok, one bedroom is too hot. Another ice cold. Your friends talk about their heating and cooling bills and YOUR's appears to be <u>way</u> too high. What's a homeowner to do? Call <u>Jones Heating and Cooling</u>. Sometimes poor heating and cooling is just the result of damaged vents and ducts. Maybe you don't have the right size unit for your home. New heating and cooling systems are much more energy efficient and save you money every month. Get to the root of your heating and cooling problem with a free estimate from <u>Jones Heating and Cooling, online at XYZ.com</u>

Contracting "Gray Thumb"

Title	Gray Thumb
Client/Product	Contracting
Voice Gender	Male or Female
Length	:30
Direction	
Suggested Music/SFX	

Joe has a gray thumb. Yes, some people have GREEN thumbs, but Joe's is gray. Oh, he still makes things grow, but not with plants...with CONCRETE! Joe Jones Contracting can make your patio grow! Need a new driveway? Joe can do that in a flash! A foundation, pathway or bigger back porch...Jones Contracting has the knowledge, skills and gray thumb to make it happen. Call or visit Jones Contracting at XXX.com and say "I need your Gray Thumb!"

Retail

Flowers "Anytime"

Title	Anytime
Client/Product	Flowers
Voice Gender	Male or Female
Length	:30
Direction	sincere
Suggested Music/SFX	Light and happy

Flowers. You gotta send them of Valentine's Day....and...maybe on Mother's Day. But what about TODAY? A beautiful floral arrangement sent for no other reason than to say "I'm thinking of you," is the perfect way to make someone's day special. Your partner, your mom...even that hard working associate. Do something special for someone special in your life...and YOU'LL feel special. Jones Flowers, we're here for you all year...including TODAY. Jones Flowers (location/number and/or website)

Jeweler "What Women Want"

Title	What Women Want
Client/Product	Jeweler
Voice Gender	Male or Female
Length	:30
Direction	conversational
Suggested Music/SFX	

Freud is well known for quoting Napoleon when he said: "What does a woman want?"

At Jones Jewelry we KNOW what women want. And we've got it.

And selecting jewelry from Jones Jewelry shows her...YOU get it.

Jones Jewelry has everything from simple styling to elegant designer fashions.

And of course, Jones Jewelry is your ultimate destination for engagement rings...I'm just sayin'.

Be a bigger hit with the ladies than Freud or that little guy from France. Visit Jones Jewelry...it's what women want.

Jones Jewelry, (location)

Market/Grocery "Katherine Valentine"

Title	Katherine
Client/Product	Market/Grocery
Voice Gender	Male
Length	:30
Direction	Overly sincere… a little over the top
Suggested Music/SFX	Romantic music. Dog bark & boat horn

Katherine is the love of my life and only want the best for her so I went to Paris for her Poodle (bark) and Yalta for her yacht (boat horn)…and for Valentine's Day I'm going to Jones Market. You see Jones Market has it all. Chocolate covered Strawberries, Champagne, beautiful flowers and those gift cards to her favorite restaurants and online stores…oh Katherine loves her gift cards. Oh, and maybe I'll pick up a steak for a romantic Valentines dinner…or… frozen pizza. Jones Market…I love you almost as much as Katherine.

Furniture Store/Decorator "Why Not Me"

Title	**Why not me?**
Client/Product	Furniture or Decorator
Voice Gender	Male or Female
Length	:30
Direction	
Suggested Music/SFX	

Grandma's dining table with 5 unmatched chairs. A sofa and a dog that seem to have fused together. And a Farrah Fawcett poster. Sound familiar? Time to reclaim your home and give it some style? Jones Furniture and Decorators can help you discover your style and bring it to life. You've drooled over those TV makeover shows and thought "Why not me?" Well, let the pros at Jones Furniture and Decorators make it happen! Visit Jones Furniture and Decorators at (location) online at XYZ.com

Mattress "Who is to Blame"

Title	Who is to blame
Client/Product	Mattress Sales
Voice Gender	Male or Female
Length	:30
Direction	
Suggested Music/SFX	

That cup of coffee after lunch. The evening news. Your Partner? What do you blame for a bad night's sleep? Maybe it's your mattress. How old IS that mattress, anyway? Right now is a great time to stop by Jones Sleep Center. Storewide specials at Jones Sleep Center make getting a good night's sleep easier than ever. Stop looking for things to blame, a good night sleep starts Jones Sleep Center (location).

Retail "Shop Local"

Title	Shop Local
Client/Product	Retail
Voice Gender	Male or Female
Length	:15
Direction	Conversational
Suggested Music/SFX	

Ok, when I need something I go on the Internet and search for a bargain. Sometimes I'm online for hours trying to save a few cents. Well, yesterday I went to JONES STORE and found just what I wanted in seconds. When I got home, out of habit I looked it up. JONES STORE had the best deal. Wow! I still go online to play Candy Crush and watch cat videos, but when I need a bargain and I need it now, my first stop is JONES STORE. Shop smarter and shop local. JONES STORE

Western Wear "Look Good"

Title	Look Good
Client/Product	Western Wear
Voice Gender	Male or Female
Length	:30
Direction	
Suggested Music/SFX	

Everything looks good in the summer. The trees look good, the skies look good...compared to winter our lawns definitely look good in the summer. Summertime is kinda like....Wranglers! Because, everyone looks good in a pair of Wrangler Jeans. Jones General Store wants YOU to look good, in your next pair of Wranglers. Finish your good look with Jones General Store's huge selection of hats, belts, shirts and boots. Whether you want to look good for work or play Jones General Store and Wrangler have just what you need. Jones General Store (Location)

Cause everyone looks good in a pair of Wranglers

"Wrangler" is used as a "place holder." May brands or products can be substituted.

Market Valentine "Your Way"

Title	Your Way
Client/Product	Market
Voice Gender	Male or Female
Length	:30
Direction	Sincere
Suggested Music/SFX	Romantic music.

A single rose and a kiss on the cheek? A gourmet home cooked dinner finished with decadent chocolate dipped strawberries? Or maybe a lovable plush toy hidden in a very unexpected place? Whatever your idea of romance is, Jones Market has it. Valentine's Day is this Saturday and Jones Market is stocked with flowers, cards, candy, chocolates and more. This Valentines Day do it YOUR way...and head to Jones Market!

Framing/Print Shops "Plain Walls"

Title	Plain Walls
Client/Product	Print/Framing
Voice Gender	Male or Female
Length	:30
Direction	
Suggested Music/SFX	

Have you got Plain Walls?

Liven up those plain walls... with art.

Picasso, Van Gogh, Rembrandt and Monet even new, up and coming artists.

Jones Gallery and Frames has fine art prints and posters waiting to give life to your plain walls. Also a great selection of frames and custom framing for your family photos and prints. Liven up your home or office. Make an impression with an impressionist. Give you plain wall a master touch with a great master Loose those Plain walls at Jones Gallery and Frames (location).

Shoe Store "Talk Show"

Title	Talk Show
Client/Product	Shoes
Voice Gender	3 females
Length	:30
Direction	
Suggested Music/SFX	

TV Host – A sophisticated Female TV Host like Tyra Banks.

Woman 1 – a mature woman similar to Meryl Streep in The Devil Wears Prada.

Woman 2 – a young woman, 18-20 years old, similar to Reece Witherspoon in Legally Blonde.

(Applause)

Host- [upbeat] **Welcome back to our show! Questions?**

Woman 1- **Yes. Where did you get those stunning designer shoes you're wearing?**

Host – [distracted] **Oh... I... got them at Jones Shoes.**

[a little more excited] **They were 50 percent off the retail price!**

[realizes she's still doing a talk show] **Uh, next question.**

Woman 2- [excited, peppy] **I totally need shoes just like those!** [skeptical] **But the shipping is the other 50 percent, right?**

Host- [diva] **Girl, they have free shipping.**

[giving in] **Ok, Jones Shoes specializes in women's shoes with over 200 designer brands we all love. And they add new styles every day. Their just down the street at (LOCATION)**

(Applause and stampede of shoes continuing throughout to end)

Host- [panicked] **Wait! The show's not over!...Forget it, I need new shoes too!**

Antique Shop "Memories"

Title	Memories
Client/Product	Antique Shop
Voice Gender	Male or Female
Length	:30
Direction	Slow and sincere
Suggested Music/SFX	Easy and older style music.

Maybe it's the sound of that clock on the mantle at Granpa's old place when you were a child. Or the special conversations you had while sipping tea from Mom's flowery teacups. Antiques are more than just objects they're reminders of special times, places and people. At Jones Antiques we sell more than beautiful antiques. We sell memories. Memories from your past and memories to come. Take some time and browse our memories at Jones Antiques, (Location).

Building Supply "Talking Lumber"

Title	Talking Lumber
Client/Product	Lumber Yard
Voice Gender	Male
Length	:30
Direction	Tough character
Suggested Music/SFX	

Sometimes I like to get hammered. But only because I'm bored. I mean, I AM a board. Yep, I'm a 2 by 4, but, of course, size doesn't matter. And if it did Jones Lumber has any size you need. Some of my lumbering buddies here at Jones Lumber have been used in an awful lot of the homes, buildings and barns in our area. I was just purchased to be a part of a new tree house. I can't wait to get nailed. Jones Lumber, we're a part of just about everything you see. Location and online at Jones Lumber dot com.

Guitar or Music Shop "We Got Your Axe"

Title	We got your axe
Client/Product	Guitar Shop or Music Shop
Voice Gender	Male or Female
Length	:30
Direction	Fun attitude
Suggested Music/SFX	Great solo guitar music

Nothing helps pass the time like a good axe
(distant voice: "TIMBER!")
Not that kind of axe. I'm talking Guitars.
(good guitar music)
<u>Jones Guitars</u> has 'em. And we're just a beat away at <u>Jones Guitars dot com</u> or drop by our shop at (Location)

And don't fret, all <u>Jones Guitars</u> are professionally setup and ready to rock.

Guitars, Amps, Lessons Repairs and oh yeah, honesty. <u>Jones Guitars</u>...Strum on in to <u>(Location)</u> or online at <u>Jones Guitars dot com</u>...Yeah, we got your axe.

Frame Shop "Dark Night"

Title	Dark Night
Client/Product	Frame Shop
Voice Gender	Male or Female
Length	:30
Direction	Like a 40s private eye (film noir)
Suggested Music/SFX	Detective music (saxophone would work)

It was a dark night. The kind that happens only when it's not daytime...then SHE walked in. She took one look at my wall and whispered, "You've been framed."

I looked her in the eyes and said, "That's right sister, I've been to Jones Frames. They can frame anything. Jones Frames does great work and they're affordable, even on a private eye's salary."

The next morning we both went to Jones Frames at Location. It was the beginning of a beautiful friendship.

Nursery/Garden Center "Talking Flowers"

Title	Talking flowers
Client/Product	Garden Center
Voice Gender	2 females & Announcer
Length	:30
Direction	
Suggested Music/SFX	

Voice 1 (excited)

Pick me! Pick Me! Pick Me!

Voice 2 (calm)

Too needy Daisy. You've got to be subtle with a little color.

Voice 1

That's easy for you to say, Rose. Everyone LOVES you. Even though you can be a little prickly sometimes.

Voice 2

Relax, everyone here at Jones Gardens ends up in great homes. And while we're here we are treated like royalty. After all we wouldn't even be at Jones Gardens if we weren't the best!

Voice 1

SHHH! Here comes someone with a gleam in their eye and green thumb!

Anncr.

Only the best flowers are waiting to be adopted at Jones Gardens (Location)

Pet/Aquarium Shop "Hi Def"

Title	Hi Def
Client/Product	Aquarium-Pet Store
Voice Gender	Male or Female
Length	:30
Direction	See script
Suggested Music/SFX	

(dramatic delivery)
High definition crystal-clear clarity.
Vivid colors.
Detailed action and drama.
(more friendly delivery)
No, I'm not talking about a widescreen TV...its something *more* exciting. Bring the beauty and wonder of world oceans and hidden rivers into your home or office...with the help of Jones Aquariums. From dramatic ocean reefs to peaceful tropical aquariums, Jones's knows the waters. So whether you're an old salt who used to crew with Cousteau or you are new to the magic of marine life, Jones Aquarium is waiting for you. Jones Aquariums Location.

Grocery "Graduation"

Title	Graduation
Client/Product	Grocery Store
Voice Gender	Male or Female
Length	:30
Direction	Sincere
Suggested Music/SFX	See script

(school bell)

That first day of school you handed them a pack with fruit and snacks from Jones Market and hid a little tear.

(Graduation music: "Pomp & Circumstance")

Now they're ready to be handed their diploma and, you know, there's going to be another tear. Then it will be time for the celebration.

(Upbeat music)

Jones market has got you covered. Graduation cakes, Party Platters, Freshly made chicken and even their favorite fruit and snacks. And don't forget a gift card. Jones Market, we've been here for you through the years and we're here for you now.

Nursery "Earth Day"

Title	Earth Day
Client/Product	Nursery
Voice Gender	Male or Female
Length	:30
Direction	
Suggested Music/SFX	Bird effects and light music.

Earth Day is Wednesday April 22 and everyone at Jones Nursery urges to take some time to make our Earth a better place. Do your part to recycle and encourage others to do the same. Take some time with your family to plant a tree, shrub or just a flower to commemorate Earth Day and our commitment to our environment. Jones Nursery at (location) working with you to make our planet a healthier and more beautiful place to live!

BBQ Grill /Hardware Store "Grilling Tips"

Title	Grilling Tips
Client/Product	BBQ store or market
Voice Gender	Male or Female
Length	:15
Direction	informative
Suggested Music/SFX	Sound of meat on a grill

Jones Shop Grilling Tip:

It's easier to brush off debris and clean your grill after it is hot, so after pre-heating your grill use a long handled wire brush.

For a complete selection of grills and accessories, drop by and see the grilling experts at Jones Shop (location.)

Jones Shop Grilling Tip:

Reduce sticking by oiling your hot grill rack with a vegetable oil soaked paper towel. Use tongs to rub it over the rack.

For a complete selection of grills and accessories, drop by and see the grilling experts at at Jones Shop (location.)

Jones Shop Grilling Tip:

Tired of vegetables and small pieces of meat falling through the grill? Try a grill basket. They are also great for flakey fish!

For a complete selection of grills and accessories, drop by and see the grilling experts at at Jones Shop (location.)

T-Shirt Shop "Classy or Crazy"

Title	Classy or Crazy
Client/Product	T-shirt Shop
Voice Gender	Male or Female
Length	:30
Direction	
Suggested Music/SFX	

Make a statement. When your softball team hits the field, you can look like classy pros...or maybe the craziest misfits in the park. That's where Jones T-Shirts comes in. From classy to crazy we can design and print traditional...and not so traditional jerseys and T-shirts. Family reunion or wedding coming up? Let Jones T Shirts make your group look like classy pros or crazy misfits. *You get the idea.* Come in with your design or let us show you ours.

Jones T-Shirts (Location/Website)

Boutique/Market "Mother's Day"

Title	Mothers Day
Client/Product	Boutique, Market ?
Voice Gender	Male or Female
Length	:30
Direction	Fun
Suggested Music/SFX	

:15

Mom likes Cat videos, flowers and chocolates...oh, she loves her chocolates. Your Jones Boutique has everything she wants for Mother's Day...well, except those cat videos. Jones Boutique, here for you, and your mom.

:15

Face it, your mom's never been that predictable. Like the time showed up unexpectedly at your front door, the time you....well...you remember...and so does mom. Give her something unexpected...from Jones Boutique.

Building/Hardware Store "After Xmas Remodel"

Title	After Xmas Remodel
Client/Product	Home Hardware
Voice Gender	Male or Female
Length	:30
Direction	Sincere
Suggested Music/SFX	Any appropriate

How was your Christmas? *(slight pause)*

Oh, I'm sure you were satisfied with festivities, family and friends…but…where you **satisfied** with your house? When guests came over where you pleased with you cabinets, floors and walls. Or did you just not invite **anyone** over because of the shape your home was in? Maybe now's the time to visit Jones Home and Hardware. Whether it's a few minor touch-ups or a long put-off remodel, Jones Home and Hardware will help get your home in shape…for the next holiday!

Book Store "Amazing Books"

Title	Amazing Books
Client/Product	Book Store
Voice Gender	Male or Female
Length	:30
Direction	Excited
Suggested Music/SFX	

It's portable. It never needs recharging. Drop it and it doesn't break. You can use it in the sun. Use it in bed. Great for home, travel or work.

And it makes the perfect gift for young and old. Of course, we're talking about the remarkable invention...THE BOOK.

Jones Books has thousands of these amazing devices waiting for you. From Classic novels to the latest best sellers. Political insight to outrageous humor. Books for kids, family and dreamers. Discover the amazing world of Books at Jones Books. LOCATION

Jeweler "Sparkle in Her Eyes"

Title	Sparkle in her eyes
Client/Product	Jeweler
Voice Gender	Male or Female
Length	:30
Direction	sincere
Suggested Music/SFX	

You always think of her as "good ole mom." So much older than you and, although you don't always admit it, wiser than you. But sometimes when her favorite song comes on the radio, you see it in her eyes. That sparkle of a carefree young girl. This Mother's Day Jones Jewelers wants you to remember "good ole mom", but also acknowledge the young girl in her heart. Jones Jewelers has a sparkling collection of rings, necklaces and pendants that will bring that sparkle to your Mom's eyes. Jones Jewelers

Grocery/Market "What Mom Didn't Do"

Title	What Mom Didn't Do
Client/Product	Grocery or Market
Voice Gender	Male or Female
Length	:30
Direction	Fun and honest
Suggested Music/SFX	

When you had that weird hairstyle in high school, Mom didn't complain...too much. When you first thought you found true love, she didn't argue. You posted that photo at 3am on Facebook and she didn't even comment, but you KNOW she saw it. This Mother's Day Jones Market wants you not just to remember all the things your mom did but also what she DIDN'T do. Just don't forget her. A card, roses, chocolates or a potted plant. You're neighborhood Jones Market is here for you...and your mom.

Medical & Such

Dentist/Oral Surgeon "Doctor Speaking"

Title	Doctor Speaking
Client/Product	Dentist Oral Surgeon
Voice Gender	Male or Female
Length	:15 & 05
Direction	Fun
Suggested Music/SFX	

:15

You love your car, right? If it had a messed up grill you'd fix it, right? Take a look in the mirror and smile. Need a little work? Fix it. I'm Dr Jones, call me at (Phone number)

:15

A real man smiles in the face of trouble. But are you afraid trouble might start laughing at you? I'm Dr Jones, let me improve your smile and your odds. Call me (Phone number)

:15

Everybody's crazy about a sharp dressed man, but make sure your smile doesn't clash with your wardrobe. I'm Dr Jones, call me and I'll give your that smile you've always wanted, (Phone number)

:05

Stop hiding behind your mustache. I'm Dr Jones, call me at (Phone number)

:05

You can't smile away your problems when your smile IS a problem, call Dr Jones at (Phone number)

:05

Overhaul your mouth. At least your smile. I'm Dr Jones, your tooth mechanic, call (Phone number)

Chiropractor "Tune Up"

Title	TUNE UP
Client/Product	Chiropractor
Voice Gender	Male or Female
Length	:30
Direction	
Suggested Music/SFX	Light music.

People that love their cars regularly take them in for a tune up because they want optimum performance. Don't YOU deserve the same treatment? Jones Chiropractic offers a full range of treatments to help your BODY reach its Optimum performance. We'll discuss your goals, give you the support you need and then you'll quickly see results. Chiropractic, Massage and Nutrition advice all at (your town)'s most welcoming chiropractic clinic. Jones Chiropractic, (location) and online at XYZ.com

Health Store "One Body"

Title	One Body
Client/Product	Health Store
Voice Gender	Male or Female
Length	:30
Direction	Informative
Suggested Music/SFX	(you might add car sputtering effects)

Imagine you've got an automobile and it has to last you the rest of your life. Would you put just any kind of oil or gasoline in it? You'd probably check with the pros about what's best. Well, the BODY you've got is the only one you'll get, so consult the pros at Jones Health about what's best for you. From vitamins to supplements, Jones Health not only stocks everything you want, they'll give you the advice you need to make smart decisions. You've only got one body, treat it right. Jones Health (location)

Body Rejuvenation/Fitness Center "Summer Body"

Title	Summer Body
Client/Product	Fitness Center or Plastic Surgeon
Voice Gender	Male or Female
Length	:30
Direction	Bright delivery
Suggested Music/SFX	Summer music, surf effects

Visualize summer…. visualize the beach…now visualize your body. Are we there yet? Get in swimsuit shape Jones Fitness Center. It takes nature millions of years to make a beach…but it only takes a quick phone to Jones Fitness center to start work on your BEACH body. Stop searching for "cover-ups" and start shopping for bikinis.

Call or drop into Jones Fitness (Address/Phone)

Dentist "Anxieties"

Title	Anxieties
Client/Product	Dentist
Voice Gender	Male or Female
Length	:30
Direction	Friendly
Suggested Music/SFX	Light music

Relaxing, gentle, caring, compassionate.

Is that what comes to mind when you think of going to the dentist?

If not, maybe you should visit Dr. Jones.

You'll smile while improving your smile. Dr. Jones and her entire team are dedicated to providing you with the personalized, gentle care you deserve. She understands your anxieties and is dedicated to fearful patients, even your anxieties about finances

Visit Dr. Jones at XYZ.com   or call XXX-XXXX... and... smile!

Walk-In Clinic "Predict"

Title	**Predict**
Client/Product	Walk in clinic
Voice Gender	Male or Female
Length	:30
Direction	Sincere
Suggested Music/SFX	Easy going.

Some things you can't predict. Like that trampoline accident on a Saturday morning, or finding out after school that someone has been feeling ill all day. Don't worry, Jones Express Clinic is there for you, seven days a week from 9am to 7pm. Make an appointment or just walk in. And at Jones Express Clinic we are here for unexpected emergencies, illness checkups, sports physicals and flu shots. Life is full of surprises but one thing you can predict...is that Jones Express Clinic is always there for you.

Elder Homecare "They Were There for You"

Title	They were there for you
Client/Product	Elder Home Care
Voice Gender	Male or Female
Length	:30
Direction	Sincere
Suggested Music/SFX	Soft sentimental

They were always there for you when you were a child. They always had the right answers. Now they could use a little help. And so could you. All is Jones Home Care knows that it is often impossible to check on loved ones after a long day at work. Jones Home Care provides carefully screened caregivers to help ease the burden of getting older. Learn more, call Jones Home Care or online at XYZ.com

Dentist "Bad Puns"

Title	Bad Puns
Client/Product	Dentist
Voice Gender	Male or Female
Length	:15
Direction	
Suggested Music/SFX	

:15

Bitten off more than you can chew?

Call <u>Dr Jones</u>. Family dentistry with pricing that's not hard to swallow.

<u>Dr Jones Dentistry.</u> (Phone and/or Location)

:15

Born with a silver spoon in your mouth?

<u>Dr Jones</u> will gladly remove it. ...or polish it.

<u>Dr Jones Dentistry.</u> (Phone and/or Location)

:15

Never look a gift horse in the mouth.

Let <u>Dr Jones</u> do it. She's an expert in mouths. And teeth!

<u>Dr Jones Dentistry.</u> (Phone and/or Location)

Vision Shop/Optometrist "Beautiful World"

Title	**Beautiful World**
Client/Product	Vision Shop
Voice Gender	3 voices
Length	:30
Direction	
Suggested Music/SFX	

#1

Voice 1. What a cute little doggie. What's its name?

Voice 2. Tiffany. It's my daughter!

Time for an eye checkup?

<u>Visit Jones Vision</u>. It's a beautiful world out that, don't miss it.

<u>Jones Vision (location and/or website)</u>

#2

Voice 1. Man it's foggy today, I better turn on the headlights.

Voice 2. It's clear as a bell! Your glasses are Waaaayy scratched up.

Time for a new pair of glasses? <u>Visit Jones Vision</u>. It's a beautiful world out that, don't miss it. <u>Jones Vision (location and/or website)</u>

Pharmacy "Cold Confusion"

Title	Cold Confusion
Client/Product	Drug Store
Voice Gender	Male or Female
Length	:30
Direction	friendly
Suggested Music/SFX	

Have you ever stood in the aisle and just stared numbly at all the remedies for the common cold. Daytime, Nightime. Antihistamine, Decongestant. Maybe a little of everything. It's can be very confusing, especially when you or your loved one is feeling sick and you don't have time to enroll in med school.

No Problem. Just drop into Jones Pharmacy. We're always here to help and offer simple explanations and give thoughtful recommendations. Jones Pharmacy, here for your health...AND here to help.

Jones Pharmacy (location)

Automotive

Auto Dealer "Uncomplicated"

Title	Uncomplicated
Client/Product	Auto Dealer
Voice Gender	Male or Female
Length	:30
Direction	Very sincere
Suggested Music/SFX	

It seems everyone is making buying a new car complicated and confusing. Everyone except Jones Auto. I kid you not, if you need a ride...or just want a better ride, don't waste your time with the other guys. Just head to Jones Auto. Nothing complicated. No hard to understand deals. No buy-one-pay-for two, your discount's in the mail gimmicks. Just simple uncomplicated fair prices on great vehicles.

Jones Auto (location) it's just that simple.

Auto Repair "Summer Campaign"

Title	Summer Campaign
Client/Product	Auto shop
Voice Gender	Female (somewhat sexy/suggestive)
Length	:30
Direction	Sexy and fun
Suggested Music/SFX	

:15

Female (somewhat sexy/suggestive))

Sometimes you just need a change...*and a rotation.*

And I know just the guys to do it. Jones Auto! Just 29.99 for an oil change and tire rotation Jones Auto (Location and website)

:15

Female (somewhat sexy/ suggestive)

No matter how hard I try, I just can't stop.(brake skid SFX)

There's only one thing to do...visit Jones Auto. For 89.99 they'll service my brakes, replace pads or shoes, and more... Jones Auto (Location and website)

:15

Female (somewhat sexy/suggestive)

Is it just me or are you starting to get hot too?

I need to visit the guys.

The guys at JONES AUTO. They'll recharge my air conditioning system and cool me down for just 79.99. Get the details at Jones Auto (Location and website)

Auto Repair "Ouch!"

Title	OUCH
Client/Product	Auto Repair
Voice Gender	Male or Female
Length	:30
Direction	Normal
Suggested Music/SFX	Sound effect of auto crash

(Crash effect)
Ouch! Not good....
What's next?
　Find a tow truck, find a body shop, get an estimate...then Wait. Then endure the hassle, then, wait even longer....ouch!
Of course, you could make just one call and avoid the "ouch!"
Call <u>Jones Auto Repair</u>
They will do your towing, give you an fair and honest estimate
They'll do the work on site...quickly and hassle free.
And you'll be back on the road..."ouch" free!
We hope you never find yourself in a... **(crash effect)**
But if you do, one call to <u>Jones Auto Repair</u> will take care of everything.
<u>Jones Auto Repair</u> at xxx-xxxx

Auto Repair "Double Talk"

Title	Double Talk
Client/Product	Auto Repair
Voice Gender	Male Mechanic Announcer (male or Female)
Length	:30
Direction	Mechanic should be a wise-guy. Almost cartoonish. Announcer is honest and conversational
Suggested Music/SFX	Sound of auto shop (air gun, power tools, etc)

(MECHANIC-talking fast) The problem with your car is ya sprung a framus on the gear-hockey. You could shim the whoodaddy with a double gerkin but Darrel and I think you need to replace all your arch supports and completely re-fulcrum your valve twisters.

(Announcer) When it comes to your car you don't need double talk. Jones Auto is known for quality and reliability and you don't get that reputation by giving your customers **double-talk**.
Jones Auto (Location) and online at XYZ.com
Whether its service or something a little more serious…get straight talk from Jones Auto…not double talk

(Mechanic) And we'll have to rotate your monkey bearings.

Auto Repair "Sorry Mechanic"

Title	**Sorry Mechanics**
Client/Product	Auto Repair Shop
Voice Gender	Male or Female
Length	:30
Direction	
Suggested Music/SFX	

Sorry that's too old

Sorry that's too new

Sorry I don't even know what country that came from?

Is "sorry" your mechanic's favorite word? At Jones Auto shop, we can handle it all. From vintage to the latest state of the art models. Foreign and domestic. Don't settle for a "sorry" mechanic. See the "Yes" guys at Jones Auto Shop. (Location)

Car Wash "I'm Filthy"

Title	I'm filthy
Client/Product	Car Wash
Voice Gender	Female
Length	:30
Direction	As if talking to significant other
Suggested Music/SFX	Traffic sounds

:30

You know, you take me for granted. I drive you anywhere you want to go...any time of the day... in any weather... but you treat me like dirt. When was the last time you paid me a compliment...well why <u>would</u> you? I'm *filthy*. I could use a little pampering. Maybe a quick trip to <u>Jones Car Wash.</u> The full "spa treatment" only takes a few minutes. You'll see the sparkle in my eyes... and my headlights. We'll both feel better about each other afterwards.

Come on...let's go to <u>Jones Car Wash at location.</u>

:30

(Honk) Hey, I saw you staring at her bumper. How come you never look at me like that anymore? You used to, until you started neglecting me. Looking gorgeous doesn't just happen, you know. I need a little TLC, the kind that comes from the gentle touch at <u>Jones Car Wash.</u> A full body shampoo... maybe a little wax job...it's totally your call. Come on, let's go to <u>Jones Car Wash </u>for old time's sake. You remember how we get there don't ya? <u>Jones Car Wash, (location)</u>

Auto Detailing "Spring Cleaning"

Title	Spring Cleaning
Client/Product	Auto Detailing
Voice Gender	Male or Female
Length	:30
Direction	
Suggested Music/SFX	

It's that time of year. Time to spruce up your home and make is shine! No not your HOUSE, your CAR, the place you call "home" for so many hours every week! Come to Jones Auto Detailing and let our pros give your automobile a thorough Spring Cleaning. A thorough hand wash, with complete detailing inside and out and our deluxe hand wax finish. Start spring out fresh, with the help from Jones Auto Detailing. Drop by (Location) or call (phone number). Jones Auto Detailing!

Auto Dealer "Freeze Out Sale"

Title	**Freeze Out Sale**
Client/Product	Auto Dealer
Voice Gender	Male or Female
Length	:30
Direction	Lots of energy
Suggested Music/SFX	Face paced

The colder it gets the hotter the deals at Jones Auto! That's right, since temperatures are low, so are our prices. Are we crazy? No…possibly a little frostbit, though…but don't call the paramedics, just put on some driving gloves and come down to Jones Auto and chill. You'll find exactly the vehicle you want. And with each new automobile you buy, we'll provide a free cup of hot coffee (Some restrictions apply, see dealer for details).

Jones Auto's FREEZE OUT SALE (location). Going on now until we thaw out and come to our senses.

Auto Body "Charm Bracelet"

Title	Charm Bracelet
Client/Product	Auto Body
Voice Gender	Male or Female
Length	:30
Direction	fun
Suggested Music/SFX	Possible auto accident sound effects

Is your automobile like a charm bracelet? That little ding on the door is a reminder of the parking lot at your sister's wedding. The chipped windshield a reminder of that vacation. That scraped bumper is a memento from…well…that's just something you don't like to talk about. Drop by Jones Auto and let us smooth out all those reminders. Minor to major body work. Windshield replacement and paint jobs. Jones Auto does it all! Drop by and see our "charm-removal-specialists", (location/website)

Auto Salvage "Pull 'em Out"

Title	**Pull em out**
Client/Product	Auto Salvage
Voice Gender	Male
Length	:30
Direction	Tough western style
Suggested Music/SFX	Rawhide music

Open em up
 Pull em out
Put em in
 Drive away....Jones Salvage
Jones Salvage, your self-service wrecking yard
Over ten acres of cars, trucks, vans and SUVs.
Jones Salvage (location)
7:30 to 4:30, Seven Days a week
You know what you want, come and get it.
Jones Salvage

Auto Dealer "No Time for Bull"

Title	No time for bull
Client/Product	Auto Dealer
Voice Gender	Male
Length	:30
Direction	Fast talking but honest -Dennis Leary style
Suggested Music/SFX	None or fast paced.

I've just got 30 seconds, so no time for bull.

Money is tight and you need to watch every penny and it no secret the auto industry wants to move cars, so let's not play games.

You need a car, we need to sell you a car. Jones Auto has lots of pre-owned cars...okay, you call them used cars. We've got em, you need one. We'll cut the price, find the financing, work out a plan....we'll make it work.

Get directions to Jones Auto at XYZ.com . Now, we need you to remember this: XYZ.com.

Rental Car "Summer Wheels"

Title	Summer Wheels
Client/Product	Rental Car
Voice Gender	Male or Female
Length	:30
Direction	Friendly
Suggested Music/SFX	upbeat

Summer means places to see, people to visit…things to do! But are your "wheels" holding you back. Not enough room to take the gang out of town? Is your "ride" not reliable enough for even a weekend getaway? <u>Jones Rental</u> has the "wheels" you need. Whether it's a gas saving economical vehicle or a more spacious 4 door model, we've got the rides and the rates to make your summer travel a reality. For your short hop out of town or something to handle visiting relatives, <u>Jones Rental</u> is your Summer Solution. <u>Jones Rental (location/website and or phone)</u>

Custom Wheel & Tires "Invention of the Wheel"

Client/Product	Custom Wheel & Tires
Voice Gender	Male, female & announcer
Length	:30
Direction	
Suggested Music/SFX	Rock chiseled, tire squeel

:30 *Invention of the Wheel*

(sound of rock being chiseled)

Announcer: Since the Stone Age....it was hard for a guy to get noticed without a little style.

Cave-Guy: I invent WHEEL!

Girl: Oooooh...polished granite!

Announcer: Nowadays it just takes a trip to Jones Wheel and Tire

Girl: Oooooh...polished chrome!

Announcer: Don't drive in the "past," roll with style on custom rims from Jones Wheel & Tire

Cave-Guy: That cheaper than mastodon poo.

Announcer: ...and shinier!

Jones Wheel & Tire, (Address) Get out of the Stone Age and in to Jones Wheel & Tire

(tire squeal out)

RV Sales & Repair "Get Out of Here"

Title	Get out of here
Client/Product	RV Sales & Repair
Voice Gender	Male or Female
Length	:30
Direction	fun
Suggested Music/SFX	

Get out of here!

I know you want to.

What's stopping you?

Need an RV or camper? Got one but it needs a little TLC or updating? Jones RV Sales & Service can put you into a great RV or camper. You should see our incredible inventory online at XYZ.com. Whether you're looking for new RV or need service Jones RV Sales & Service is here for YOU. Visit Jones RV Sales & Service at (Location) then….GET OUT OF HERE!

Miscellaneous

Boutique or ANY "Not ONE Thing I Like"

Title	Not ONE thing I like
Client/Product	Boutique or ANY
Voice Gender	Male or Female
Length	:30
Direction	
Suggested Music/SFX	

Is there one thing I like about Jones Boutique?

Nope, *not one single thing*.

How could there be, they have so much to like. That's where I got my awesome one of a kind (NAME OF ITEM OR PRODUCT) …whoops, that was supposed to be my little secret. That (ITEM) that my son loves and that (ITEM) that I gave to Annette on her birthday, I purchased them both from Jones Boutique. Nope, I say there's just not ONE thing I like about Jones Boutique, (location)

ANY "Subliminal"

Title	Subliminal
Client/Product	Any Client
Voice Gender	Male or Female
Length	:30
Direction	Normal sincere read but whisper the ()
Suggested Music/SFX	

Whisper what is in the ()...like Kevin Nealon

Research has shown that subliminal messages in advertising (Jones Services) are more effective than traditional methods because the listener doesn't even realize (Jones Services) that they're being advertised to. Apparently, you can easily promote something (Jones Services) and we will remember it. (Best XYZ in town). Hard to believe (Quick location) Weird, right?

Wine/Liquor Store "World of Wines"

Title	World of Wines
Client/Product	Wine, Liquor Store or market
Voice Gender	Male or Female
Length	:30
Direction	
Suggested Music/SFX	Elegant music.

The old-world charm of Tuscany.

Historic vineyards of France.

The excitement of Napa Valley.

The exotic tastes of South America. Isn't it time you started your world tour? Begin your journey at Jones Wines. Break out of your routine and tour the world of wines we have available. From amazing reds to crisp whites, sparkling wines for celebrating and dessert wines to end a perfect meal. There's a world of wines waiting for you at Jones Wines (Location) Your neighborhood source for great wines.

Fitness Center "Fireworks"

Title	Fireworks
Client/Product	Fitness Center
Voice Gender	Male or Female
Length	:30
Direction	Enthusiastic
Suggested Music/SFX	Uptempo music

(firework sfx)

There's only one thing better than fireworks in the night-sky...and that's the fireworks in other people's eyes when they see the new improved YOU!

Sparkle bright this July with the help of **Jones Fitness Center.** We'll help tailor a plan to get you into the shape you've been dreaming of... and, just imagine the fireworks in your OWN eyes when you see the results when you look in the mirror! Drop by today and start looking a feeling better tomorrow! **Jones Fitness Center (Location/Phone or Website)**

Appliances "Dream TV Home"

Title	Dream Home
Client/Product	Appliance Distributor
Voice Gender	Male or Female
Length	:30
Direction	
Suggested Music/SFX	

You're watching your favorite home decorating show, or maybe a tour of a celebrity's home, and the house is filled with the latest appliances and fixtures. Where do they find those products? You know you've never seen them at a hardware store. You want to know a secret? Your dream kitchen, bath or wine cellar is waiting for you at JONES APPLIANCES. Come in with your dream and we'll show you the special appliances and fixtures to make it a reality. We carry everything from high end premium brands to everyday competitively priced products. Jones Appliances (Location)

Pools "Splash"

Title	Splash
Client/Product	Pool Contractor
Voice Gender	Male or Female
Length	:30
Direction	
Suggested Music/SFX	Splash effect. Tropical music

(Splash effect)

Hear that? That's the sound of you taking your first dive into your Jones Pool.

(Splash effect)

That's your next door neighbor. He brought over a case of beer to help celebrate your new Jones Pool

(Splash effect)

Ouch! That was Uncle Lester doing a belly flop. That's gonna leave a mark.

Act now to get your new Jones Pool ready for summer fun.

(Splash effect)

What will happen in YOUR Jones Pool?

Jones Pools, (location and/or website)

Pools "All Dried Up"

Title	All dried up
Client/Product	Pools
Voice Gender	Male or Female
Length	:30
Direction	fun
Suggested Music/SFX	Splash sound effect

Are you all dried up? I mean, is your backyard a barren dessert with no escape from the summer's heat? Maybe it's time to make a splash! (SPLASH SFX)

Jones Pools can turn your backyard into an oasis. Talk to the water-fun experts at Jones Pools about your options. From a fun outdoor spa to a neighborhood-party-central-pool!!

You know you want to make a splash (SPLASH SFX)

Go ahead! Jones Pools (location and/or website)

Credit Union "YOU Can Join"

Title	YOU Can join
Client/Product	Credit Union
Voice Gender	Male or Female
Length	:30
Direction	conversational
Suggested Music/SFX	

I always heard people who belonged to credit unions brag about their great auto loans, free checking, amazing home equity loans and how everyone at the credit union treated them like a friend. Must be nice I thought. I'm not eligible, I thought. But I was wrong! You can join Jones Credit Union if you live, work or attend school in our County. So I did and boy the difference is AMAZING.

Go see me new friends at Jones Credit Union, or go to their website XYZ dot com.

Metal Recycling "A Lot of "*crap"

Title	A lot of *crap
Client/Product	Metal Recycling
Voice Gender	Male or Female (two voices)
Length	:30
Direction	
Suggested Music/SFX	Beep and cash register effects

Instructions for #rap: Record the word "crap" but bleep out the first part with a tone

V1: Cash for Scrap!
V2: *Cash for #rap?*
V1: No Cash for SCRAP
V2: *That's even better.*
Whether it's a 10 pound bag of aluminum cans or scrap metal and machinery from your worksite Jones Recycling can handle it and wants to give you money for it. Steel, iron, brass, aluminum, copper, stainless steel... we want it. Jones Recycling can unload heavy machinery and equipment.
V2: *That's a lot of #rap, I mean scrap.*
V1: Jones Recycling (location and website)

Bowling "Memories"

Title	Memories
Client/Product	Bowling
Voice Gender	Male or Female
Length	:30
Direction	
Suggested Music/SFX	Bowling effects

Remember that night you rolled three strikes in a row?
(bowling strike effect)
What about that time you bet Rachel a burger you'd make that spare then rolled a gutter ball?
(effect)
How about that great birthday party with the kids
(effect)
Isn't it time you got back on the lanes? Make new memories this week at Jones Lanes. Everyone loves to bowl...so what are you waiting for?
Jones Lanes (location)

Limo "We Keep Secrets"

Title	We keep secrets
Client/Product	Limo
Voice Gender	Male or Female
Length	:30
Direction	Up and fun
Suggested Music/SFX	Party/dance music

Imagine your dream club with your favorite beverages, the perfect mood lighting, YOUR kind of music and your closest friends*.

Now, put it on WHEELS!

Jones Limo is ready to roll for you. It doesn't matter where you're going...you're already there in a Jones Limo!

Where would you go and what would you do in your Jones Limo? Don't worry, we keep secrets!

Jones Limo, online at XYZ.com or Call 555-5555!

(If they feature a party bus or huge limo, you might want to add something like "30 of your closest friends")

Cleaners "Holiday Stains"

Title	Holiday Stains
Client/Product	Cleaners
Voice Gender	Male or Female
Length	:30
Direction	Start matter-of-fact...then more concerned
Suggested Music/SFX	Sound of bell "Ding" and buzzer.

Your famous three-bean dip with cheese (ding) Check!

That on-of-kind gift for the hostess (ding) Check!

Your perfect holiday outfit (buzzer) What's that?!

Is that a stain from last year? Looks like bean dip! Better get to <u>Jones Cleaners.</u> They're the experts in removing ugly stains from ugly sweaters...and making sure everything you wear for the holidays looks spectacular. So before and AFTER your holiday celebrations, don't forget to stop by <u>Jones Cleaners at Location</u>....and this year, be careful with the dip!

Locksmith "More than Computers"

Title	More than computers
Client/Product	Locksmith and or Security Firm
Voice Gender	Male or Female
Length	:30
Direction	Serious
Suggested Music/SFX	Corporate style music

There's a lot of talk these days about Computer and Internet security, but what about the security of your physical property at work and home. Jones Locksmith and Security is (your area)'s premiere security experts providing a full range of residential, commercial and automotive locksmith services including design & implementation of alarm systems, closed circuit TV and digital access systems. Keeping secure is requires more than just resetting your laptop password, Trust the knowledge and reputation of Jones Locksmith & Security. Online at XYZ.com

Karate School "Every Advantage"

Title	**Every Advantage**
Client/Product	Karate School
Voice Gender	Male or Female
Length	:30
Direction	
Suggested Music/SFX	Oriental Music

You want to give your child every advantage and provide them the skills to better themselves. Skills like socialization, respect, self-control and progressive achievements through discipline and exercise. Those are the cornerstones of every class at Jones Karate School. Not only are classes at Jones Karate rewarding, your child will get at "kick" out of it! Sign up today for our affordable classes. Also ask about Jones Karate School's after-school program. Online at XYZ.com

Weight Loss "New Year"

Title	New Year
Client/Product	Weight Loss
Voice Gender	Male or female (+ 1 voice for 1 line)
Length	:30
Direction	
Suggested Music/SFX	(traffic/car horns) and Bright music

Voice 1: Some things you can't change…like rush hour traffic *(traffic/car horn)* or a stubborn person's mind.

Voice 2: Forget the facts, I KNOW I'm right!

Voice 1: But one thing you CAN change is YOU! 2015 is a New Year and time for a NEW Body! <u>Jones Weight Loss Clinic</u> is offering a New Year special on their proven weight loss program. Just $(price) get's you started on the <u>change</u> you've been wanting. Don't let another New Year's resolution go unfulfilled. Call <u>Jones Weight Loss Clinic</u> at XXX-XXXX or online at XYZ/com

About the Author

David K. Jones started out in radio at the age of 15 in Lubbock, Texas. It wasn't long before he was hosting a morning show and writing scripts for commercials. His career took him across the country hosting radio shows (mostly "morning shows") in Phoenix, Seattle, Miami, Chicago and Los Angles.

He lives in Florida where he writes scripts for radio, TV and Internet projects along with voicing commercials, video games and documentaries.

David is also a watercolor artist. His paintings reflect the tropical life he loves, usually in a humorous manner.

www.ingramcontent.com/pod-product-compliance
Lightning Source LLC
Chambersburg PA
CBHW030015190526
45157CB00016B/2796